OUR HEAVENLY MOTHER

**Signs of Our Blessed Mother's Love
When the Queen of Heaven
Appeared on Earth**

●

**Guadalupe
Lourdes
Fatima**

●

By

Rev. Lawrence G. Lovasik, S.V.D.
Divine Word Missionary

CATHOLIC BOOK PUBLISHING CO.
NEW JERSEY

CONTENTS

Part 1: Our Lady of Guadalupe

The Indian Peoples of Mexico 3
Juan Diego Was an Indian Convert 5
A Beautiful Woman Appears 7
The Virgin Mary Speaks to Juan 8
The Lady Appears Again 10
The Bishop Asks for a Sign 12
Mary Arranges the Roses 14
Mary Leaves Her Own Picture 16
The Picture Is Brought to the Cathedral 19
Mother of the Americas 20

Part 2: Our Lady of Lourdes

Member of a Loving Catholic Family 21
Bernadette Sees a Lady in the Grotto 22
Crowds of People Go to the Grotto 25
The Lady Gives Bernadette Her Name 27
Bernadette Tells the Lady's Name 28
Bernadette Enters the Convent 31
Bernadette Becomes Bedridden 33
The Death of Bernadette 34
Lourdes Today 36
A Sign of Mary's Love 38

Part 3: Our Lady of Fatima

An Angel Appears to Three Children 39
A Beautiful Lady Appears 41
The Lady Comes Again 43
The Promise of a Miracle 44
The Lady of the Rosary 47
The Miracle of the Sun 48
The Deaths of Francisco and Jacinta 51
Lucia in a Convent 52
The Basilica at Fatima 54
Through Mary to Jesus 56

NIHIL OBSTAT: Francis J. McAree, S.T.D., Censor Librorum
IMPRIMATUR: ✠ Patrick J. Sheridan, D.D., Vicar General, Archdiocese of New York

The Nihil Obstat and Imprimatur are official declarations that a book or pamphlet is free of doctrinal or moral error. No implication is contained therein that those who have granted the Nihil Obstat and Imprimatur agree with the contents, opinions, or statements expressed.

(T-272)

© 1997 by Catholic Book Publishing Co., N.J.
Printed in China

Part 1: OUR LADY OF GUADALUPE

The Indian Peoples of Mexico

One of the oldest civilizations in the world was developed by the Indian peoples in Mexico. They worshiped creatures of nature and idols of their own making for they had never heard the Gospel message.

Spanish explorers arrived in Mexico around the year 1500. When they saw the beautiful silver and gold jewelry, decorated pottery, and woven rugs, many of them thought of a way to get rich.

Before long Cortez began the conquest of Mexico. The Indians were easily defeated and brutally treated. Their homes and temples were plundered and many were slain.

Juan Diego is instructed by a Franciscan missionary.

Juan Diego Was an Indian Convert

Many priests and religious accompanied the Spanish expedition to Mexico. But while the military leaders sought to establish the authority of Spain in the region, the goal of the missionaries was to win souls for Christ.

The Indians hated the invaders of their land. So the task of instructing them in the Christian Faith was made much more difficult because of the cruelty of the soldiers. How could the priests tell the natives about a loving God when the Christian soldiers showed so little mercy?

Some understanding of the conditions in which the Indians lived is important. For within ten years of the conquest of Mexico, the Mother of God would come to help these oppressed people.

Gradually the Indians learned to trust the missionaries. Many embraced the Christian Faith. And schools and Churches were built.

One of the early converts was an Aztec Indian, Juan Diego. He lived in a village just north of the present Mexico City. His wife died and Juan was living with an uncle who also became a Christian.

Among the rock ruins Juan sees a woman.

A Beautiful Woman Appears

Juan, like the other early converts, went to Mass on Saturdays in honor of the Virgin Mary. After Mass, they were instructed in the Faith.

One Saturday in 1531, just before sunrise, Juan was on his way to Mass. It was December, the Feast of the Immaculate Conception.

Suddenly he heard a woman's voice calling, "Juan Diego! Juanito!" Juan was startled and looked all around but no one could be seen. As he continued on his way he climbed a hill—and there she was!

Among the rocks he saw an Indian girl. She appeared to be about sixteen years old. She was very beautiful, dressed in a colorful cape, and surrounded by golden beams of light.

This hillside called Tepeyac had a special meaning for the Indians. Many years before a temple was built there to honor the mother of a pagan god.

Soon Juan would learn of Our Lady's desire to have a church built there in honor of the Mother of the true God.

The Virgin Mary Speaks to Juan

Juan could hardly believe his eyes. And as he drew closer, the beautiful Lady spoke to him in his native language. "Where are you going?" she asked.

"I am on my way to Holy Mass," he answered.

She said: "Dear son, I love you. I am the Virgin Mary, Mother of God, Who created all things.

"I desire that a church be built in this place where I will show my compassion to your people and to all who sincerely ask my help in their work and in their sorrows. Here I will console them. So hurry to the city and tell the Bishop all that you have heard and seen."

Juan fell to his knees on the hill called Tepeyac and said, "Noble Lady, I will do what you ask."

He had never journeyed to Mexico City before. For he was fearful of the Spaniards who had their military headquarters there. But Juan was determined to obey the beautiful woman who called herself the Virgin Mary, Mother of God. So he hurried on his way to Mexico City to see the Bishop.

Juan falls on his knees before the Virgin.

The Lady Appears Again

Upon arriving in Mexico City, Juan entered the residence of Bishop Juan Zummarraga. He told the Bishop about the vision of the beautiful Lady. And he repeated everything she said, especially her desire that a church be built there.

The Bishop could see that Juan was sincere. But he wondered why the Virgin Mother would want a church in a desert area where no one lived. He told Juan he would consider the request and that Juan should come back some other time.

Juan returned to the hill where the Lady appeared. And she was waiting for him.

So he told her about his visit to the Bishop. Juan felt unworthy to be the messenger of this beautiful Lady. But she assured him that he was the one she chose.

And she said, "Return to the Bishop tomorrow and repeat my request for a church in this place."

Once again Juan said that he would do what she asked. But he feared that the Bishop would not be pleased to see him again so soon.

Juan kneels at the feet of the Holy Virgin.

The Bishop Asks for a Sign

The next day Juan went to see the Bishop again and told him that the Lady repeated her request to have a church built.

After some thought, the Bishop told Juan to ask the Lady for a sign before he would begin building a church for her.

Back at the hill, Juan told the Holy Virgin about the Bishop's request for a sign. She directed him to return at daybreak the next day, and she would give him a sign.

When Juan arrived home, he found that his uncle was very sick with a high fever. Juan took care of him all night and the next day, so he was unable to meet the Holy Virgin.

Then when Juan was on his way to ask a priest to bring the Sacraments to his uncle, the Virgin Mother appeared. He told her "I could not meet you yesterday. My uncle is dying and needs a priest."

The Holy Virgin replied that she had already cured his uncle. Then she said, "Now go to the top of the hill and cut the flowers growing there and bring them to me."

Juan tells the Bishop what the Lady said.

Mary Arranges the Roses

Juan had promised to do whatever the Virgin Mother asked. But he still wondered how his uncle could have been cured so soon. And how could he find flowers on that rocky hill in December? He never saw flowers there before in winter.

But when he reached the top of the hill his heart leapt with joy. There among the rocks were the most beautiful roses Juan had ever seen.

Juan wore a "tilma" which was an apron used by the Aztecs. Made of coarse burlap-like fabric, it could also be used as a cape. He gathered the roses and filled his apron. Then he hurried to bring them to the Holy Virgin.

The Virgin Mother took the roses and arranged them with her own hands. Then she tied the tilma behind Juan's neck covering the roses.

"This is my sign to the Bishop," she told Juan. "Let no one see what you are carrying. Tell the Bishop that I cured your uncle. And that I myself have arranged these roses. This time he will believe you."

So Juan set out to see the Bishop once more.

Juan fills the apron with the fragrant roses.

Mary Leaves Her Own Picture

When the Bishop saw Juan coming up the road, he called in witnesses to hear Juan's story. Juan told them how he found the roses, about his uncle's cure, and the Holy Virgin's message to the Bishop.

Then he untied his tilma and the roses fell to the floor. Now a more wondrous sign was seen. For imprinted on the front of his tilma was a picture of the Virgin Mother in all her beauty just as Juan had seen her in his visions!

The Bishop and everyone with him fell to their knees. They were convinced that the Lady who appeared to Juan was really the Mother of God. Then word came from Juan's uncle that the Virgin Mother said the image on the tilma should be called "Our Lady of Guadalupe."

When the Bishop heard this he was puzzled. "Guadalupe" meant "stone serpent trodden on." Then he remembered God's word to the serpent after the fall of Adam and Eve: "There will be enmities between you and the woman; she shall crush your head." This referred to the Immaculate Conception. She would crush his head through her Son, the Redeemer of the world.

The Bishop and the others fall to their knees.

The tilma is put on display in the cathedral.

The Picture Is Brought to the Cathedral

News of the Virgin Mary's picture miraculously imprinted on the tilma spread throughout the country. And the following day the tilma was carried in a joyful procession to the cathedral where it was put on display.

Huge crowds, many of them Indian converts, came to pray to the Mother of God. And when the Indians learned that they would soon have their own church built on the site of the apparitions, hundreds volunteered to help. Within two weeks the small church was completed. And the sacred Image was placed above the altar.

As the Indians danced about in joy, one young man fell on a spear and severed his neck. Soon he was near death. His companions brought him before the Image of the Virgin of Guadalupe and begged her to help him. Within minutes he leaped to his feet as if nothing happened. Many other miracles occurred in the weeks that followed.

The Image of the Virgin Mary would remain on the tilma for centuries to come to remind all people of her love for them.

Mother of the Americas

The sacred Image of Our Lady of Guadalupe is truly "America's Treasure." And Mary is the "Mother of the Americas."

As the number of pilgrims who came to Tepeyac increased, a new shrine was built in 1709. And recently a large Basilica has been constructed to hold the vast crowds that come to honor Mary.

Popes throughout the centuries, including Pope John Paul II, have honored Mary under her title of Our Lady of Guadalupe. Her Feast Day is celebrated on December 12.

Part 2: OUR LADY OF LOURDES

Member of a Loving Catholic Family

Bernadette, who was born in 1844, lived in Lourdes, France in a loving Christian family. Her parents were very poor. And as the eldest child, she cared for her younger brothers and sisters while her parents worked in the fields.

Since she often missed going to school, when Bernadette was fourteen years old she could neither read nor write. And she had not yet made her First Communion.

When very young, Bernadette developed asthma. And she was sickly all her life. But God and the Blessed Virgin had special plans for her.

Bernadette Sees a Lady in the Grotto

It was Thursday, February 11, 1858. Bernadette, with her younger sister and her playmate, went to gather firewood. The younger girls ran on ahead, wading across the Gave River.

Bernadette heard a rustling sound. Looking at the trees by the river's edge, she saw that they were not moving. Then she caught sight of a nearby cave filled with a golden light. And she beheld a beautiful Lady.

The Lady was dressed in a white robe with a blue sash and a veil over her head. On top of each of her feet was a yellow rose. And she held a Rosary in her hands.

The Lady smiled at Bernadette and asked her to say the Rosary with her. Then she vanished. On the way home Bernadette told her companions about seeing the beautiful Lady and asked them not to tell anyone about it.

But Bernadette went back to the cave the next Sunday. She felt drawn to the place although she did not know who the Lady was.

Bernadette sees a very beautiful Lady.

Crowds of people follow Bernadette to the grotto.

Crowds of People Go to the Grotto

On Bernadette's third visit to the grotto of Massabielle, the Lady asked her to come there every day for fifteen days. Then the Lady told her to tell the priests to build a chapel there. Bernadette told this to her parish priest.

The Lady also told Bernadette to drink from the stream—pointing to a trickle of water nearby. Bernadette scraped the ground until she was able to get a sip of water. Then the Lady vanished.

For fifteen days Bernadette went to the grotto as the Lady asked her. And she talked with her. She saw the Lady only a few more times, and after July, never again. In most of her appearances, the Lady told Bernadette to wash in the stream and have a chapel built there.

During February as Bernadette was making her daily visits to the cave, crowds of people followed her. They watched as she did the things the Lady told her to do—praying the Rosary and scraping the soil until a spring gushed forth.

Bernadette was questioned often as to what she saw, what the Lady was like, and what she said. She always gave the same answers.

The Lady tells Bernadette, "I am the Immaculate Conception."

The Lady Gives Bernadette Her Name

Altogether, Bernadette saw the Lady eighteen times. On many occasions the Lady told her to pray to God for sinners.

Indeed Bernadette was chosen to tell the world that people must pray and do penance and come back to God. The message of Lourdes is prayer, penance, and conversion of life.

The famous spring at Lourdes is a reminder of the necessity of purification—the conversion of life that the Lady said was so necessary.

The Lady also wanted to bring help for the sick. From the very beginning countless numbers of sick people have been cured by washing or being immersed in this water.

Many times Bernadette asked the Lady who she was. The Lady would only smile and say nothing. Then when the beautiful Lady appeared on March 25, she answered the question by saying, "I am the Immaculate Conception."

Bernadette ran all the way to the church to tell this to the pastor.

Bernadette Tells the Lady's Name

"She said, 'I am the Immaculate Conception,'" Bernadette cried out as she burst into the room where Abbé Peyramale was sitting.

"The Lady at the cave said, 'I am the Immaculate Conception,'" she repeated.

The Abbé said, "No one can have a name like that. Do you know the meaning of those words?"

Bernadette shook her head. "I am only telling you what the Lady told me. And I've said the words over and over so that I would be sure to get them right."

The Abbé told her, "Go home now, my child. I will speak to you another time." Afterward, he reported to the Bishop all that had happened.

Some time later, in 1860, Bernadette was called to appear before the Bishop's commission, which was investigating the accounts of the apparitions at Lourdes. Bishop Laurence asked Bernadette to tell them once more what happened when she asked the Lady her name.

Bernadette was now sixteen years old, and as she answered, her face glowed. She lifted her eyes to heaven and stated, "She said, 'I am the Immaculate Conception.'"

As the Bishop looked at her radiant face, he said to the others, "Did you see that child? Did you see her face?"

And in January 1862 the commission announced its conclusion, that the Mother of God has indeed appeared to Bernadette.

Bernadette becomes a novice.

Bernadette Enters the Convent

Bernadette's life was now completely changed as news of the apparitions at Lourdes spread. She was surrounded by those who wanted to hear her speak about the visions.

So she enrolled in the school run by the Sisters of Nevers in Lourdes. She studied there for five years and learned how to read and write.

Six years later Bernadette entered the convent of the Sisters of Charity at Nevers leaving Lourdes forever. Now she began to live a hidden life. As a novice she was given the name Sister Marie-Bernard. And she lovingly served her sick and disabled sisters in the infirmary.

Her other assignment was to assist in the sacristy. As she went about her duties, her heart was filled with joy at being so near to her Eucharistic Lord.

When speaking about her faults, she humbly admitted, "I have a sharp tongue and a quick temper. And of course I want to give orders." Bernadette was a model novice spending much of her free time in prayer.

Bernadette cares for the sick in the convent infirmary.

Bernadette Becomes Bedridden

Because of Bernadette's fame, the Reverend Mother would treat her harshly at times to teach her humility.

Bernadette simply said, "The Virgin used me as a broom to remove dust. When the work is done the broom is put behind the door again."

Bernadette had always been delicate. While in the convent, she received the Anointing of the Sick three times. In the last year of her life, when only thirty-five years old, she endured great suffering. She became bedridden with asthma, tuberculosis, severe bleeding, and a tumor of the knee.

Many nights she gasped for breath. And during the day she wanted to be up and at work. Then she learned to say, "I am at my work." And when asked, "What is it?" she would answer, "Being sick."

So clear was her memory of the beauty of the Virgin Mary, that Bernadette said from her sick bed, "When you have seen her once, you just long to die so that you can see her again." Bernadette's longing would soon come true.

The Death of Bernadette

On December 8 Bernadette went to chapel with the community for the last time. When confined to her bed, she said, "When one is a bride of Jesus Christ, in any pain one must say only 'yes, my God,' without any hesitation."

And she told one sister who was caring for her, "Do not pay any attention to my suffering. I'm prepared to put up with anything for Jesus, anything to help save sinners."

She was anointed on March 20. A few weeks later as two sisters knelt at her side praying the "Hail Mary" Bernadette joined in. Her last words were, "Mother of God . . . pray for me . . . poor sinner." This was on April 16, 1879, when she was thirty-six years old.

Her body was placed in a new tomb built beneath the chapel of Saint Joseph that stood in the garden. In 1908 as part of the process leading to canonization her body was exhumed. It was found to be incorrupt.

On December 8, 1933 (Feast of the Immaculate Conception), Bernadette was declared a Saint.

Bernadette dies saying, "Holy Mary, Mother of God."

Lourdes Today

Lourdes has been a magnet attracting Christians from the very beginning. Many have come to bathe in the water seeking a cure for diseased and disabled bodies. And there have been a number of miraculous healings that were well documented. But the countless numbers of souls that have been healed by bathing in the waters at Lourdes will never be known.

In 1871 the Church of the Immaculate Conception was built over the grotto. And in 1889 the Church of the Holy Rosary was opened. Then in 1958, the Basilica of Saint Pius X was consecrated. Each year more than four million visitors come to Lourdes.

Every day in keeping with the message of Lourdes—prayer, penance, and conversion of life—everyone has ample opportunity for spiritual healing and growth. Holy Mass is celebrated throughout the day. There are communal penitential services along with individual confessions. The infirm receive the Anointing of the Sick.

Thus Lourdes brings to the world the Good News of Jesus Christ by living the message of Our Lady transmitted through Bernadette.

The Basilica of the Immaculate Conception and the Holy Rosary.

A Sign of Mary's Love

The apparitions of Mary are a sign of her active presence in the life of the Church and of her maternal love for the brothers and sisters of her Son who still journey on earth.

Their purpose is not to reveal something new but to recall and focus on some aspect of the Gospel. At Lourdes her message was prayer, penance, and conversion.

And Bernadette was the one chosen by the Blessed Virgin Mary to announce the message at Lourdes. She is now with the "beautiful Lady" that she loved and served so well.

Part 3: OUR LADY OF FATIMA

An Angel Appears to Three Children

The apparitions of the Virgin Mary at Fatima occurred during the First World War in the summer of 1917. Most of the inhabitants of this tiny village in Portugal were poor farmers. And children usually took care of herding the sheep.

The children who saw Mary were Lucia Santos, ten years old, and her cousins Francisco and Jacinta Marto, eight and six.

In the summer of 1916 an Angel appeared to them. He asked them to pray for sinners and for peace, and to bear the suffering the Lord would send them.

The children see a beautiful Lady.

A Beautiful Lady Appears

On Sunday May 13, 1917, the children were with their sheep in a field called the Cova. After lunch they said the Rosary and then began to play. Suddenly out of the clear sky two flashes of lightning appeared. The children were afraid.

The lightning drew the children's attention to a brilliant figure appearing over the trees of the Cova da Iria. It was a beautiful Lady surrounded by light. Her clothing was pure white, and a mantle edged with gold covered her head. A gold cord hung around her neck, and a pearl Rosary hung from her right arm.

The Lady smiled somewhat sadly as she said, "Have no fear. I come from heaven. I want you to come here on the thirteenth of each month, until October. Then I will tell you who I am." Then she told the children they would have much to suffer.

That evening at supper, Jacinta told her mother what happened, but she did not believe Jacinta. As word of the apparition spread, relatives came to the house wanting to know why the children were telling such lies. Lucia's mother also did not believe Lucia's story.

The Lady asks the children to say the Rosary.

The Lady Comes Again

On June 13, as the Lady had requested, the children led their flock to the Cova. They knelt down and began to say the Rosary.

As a flash of lightning came from the clear sky, Lucia cried out, "The Lady is coming."

Once again the Lady appeared surrounded in a bright light. She asked the children to say the Rosary every day for the conversion of sinners and an end to the war.

Then she told them to say after each mystery: "Oh Jesus, forgive us our sins, save us from the fire of hell. Take all souls to heaven, and especially those most in need of Your mercy."

When Lucia asked the Lady if she would take them to heaven, she replied, "Francisco and Jacinta soon. But you must remain on earth to spread the devotion of my Immaculate Heart."

When the Lady appeared for the third time on July 13, over 5,000 people were present.

The message of Fatima recalls that of Lourdes. Mary urges prayers for sinners, recitation of the Rosary, and works of penance.

The Promise of a Miracle

As Lucia, Francisco, and Jacinta were on their way to the Cova on August 13, suddenly the mayor's horse and carriage blocked the road.

He questioned them for a long time. And he even put them in jail to try to make them change their story. But the children kept repeating what truly happened and so they were released.

On that day, although the children could not come to the Cova, more than 15,000 people were there, praying the Rosary. At noon there was lightning and thunder. Then a glowing cloud settled over the tree where the Lady usually appeared.

About 30,000 people gathered at the Cova on September 13. When the Lady appeared, she asked the children to keep praying for peace.

All the apparitions of the Lady were only visible to the children. But this day the whole crowd saw a shower of white petals fall from the sky only to melt just before reaching the ground.

Lucia asked the Lady if she would give a sign that the children were telling the truth. The Lady promised a miracle would occur on October 13.

The mayor asks the children many questions.

The children kneel in the mud and pray.

The Lady of the Rosary

On October 13, a crowd estimated at 70,000 filled the Cova. They all were hoping to see the Lady. Heavy rain turned the area into a sea of mud. And at noon as the children knelt to pray the Rosary, a bolt of lightning flashed.

Once more the Lady appeared to the children in all her radiant beauty. Lucia asked the Lady, "Who are you and what do you want?" The Lady replied, "I am the Lady of the Rosary. I have come to warn the faithful to amend their lives and ask pardon for their sins. People must not continue to offend the Lord, Who is already so deeply offended. And they must say the Rosary."

Then the Lady asked that a church be built at the place where she appeared. And she promised that the war would end within a year if people would amend their lives.

She then appeared to the children in several different ways. First they saw her clothed in a blue mantle with Saint Joseph. Next the Lady was seen as the Mother of Sorrows. Jesus, dressed in a red robe, stood at her side. Finally, the children beheld her as Our Lady of Mount Carmel.

The Miracle of the Sun

A strange celestial phenomenon took place on that day, October 13. The sun seemed to fall from the sky and crash toward the earth. It was a frightening experience. And this remarkable event was witnessed by the huge crowd, not just the children. This miracle of the sun has been verified by the statements of many witnesses over the years. This is how it was reported at the time.

It was a day of heavy rains and strong winds. The weather forecast predicted no chance of clearing until the morrow. All at once the clouds parted and a brilliant sun appeared. Then the sun revolved three times within a few minutes while casting off shafts of eerie light upon earth and sky.

Moments later it appeared as if the sun was tumbling with tremendous speed toward the earth. Everyone held his breath. It stopped abruptly, changed directions, and seemed to go back into the sky. The people were terrified. And as the crowd slowly dispersed, many could be heard asking God for forgiveness.

All left with their minds filled with the message the Lady delivered through the children.

The sun seems to revolve three times.

Francisco makes his First Communion on his deathbed.

The Deaths of Francisco and Jacinta

In all of the appearances of the Blessed Virgin in the Cova at Fatima, all three children saw her. But Francisco did not hear her words.

Our Lady had foretold that Francisco and Jacinta would soon go home to heaven. And Francisco died of influenza on April 4, 1919.

Francisco made his First Communion just before he died. He had been faithful to the wishes of the Blessed Virgin. For he said many Rosaries each day and made sacrifices to atone for sinners ever since the first vision.

A short while later, Jacinta became ill. She was comforted in a special way by the Blessed Virgin who appeared to her several times. She, too, was faithful to the requests of Our Lady of Fatima. Jacinta died in a hospital in Lisbon on February 20, 1920.

When her coffin was opened in 1935, her body was found to be incorrupt.

Francisco and Jacinta are now buried in the large Basilica of Our Lady of Fatima. The cause of their beatification has begun in Rome.

Lucia in a Convent

Now Lucia alone was entrusted to spread the message of Fatima. She always remained faithful to the wishes of the Blessed Virgin Mary. And to please her, Lucia sought to live a life of holiness as an example of the spirit of the message she received from Mary.

In 1921, Lucia left Fatima to help poor children in an orphanage. Then, in 1925, she entered the Convent of the Sisters of Saint Dorothy where she was called Sister Mary Lucia of Sorrows. In 1948, she became a Carmelite nun.

At Fatima Our Lady told the children that her heart is the hope of the world. In a vision to Sister Lucia, she asked for the spread of devotion to her Immaculate Heart.

In 1930, the Bishop of Leira declared the apparitions to the children at Fatima as worthy of belief. In 13 years since the Virgin Mary had first appeared, over 200 cures had taken place there.

And Pope Pius XII approved devotion to Our Lady of Fatima and consecrated the world to her Immaculate Heart in 1943.

Lucia becomes a nun.

The Basilica at Fatima

A large Basilica has been built in Fatima at the place where the Virgin Mary appeared to the children. And thousands of pilgrims come each year from all over the world to honor the Blessed Virgin. Over the years the Popes have shown exceptional devotion to Our Lady of Fatima.

Crowds comparable to those at Lourdes are common. In a rustic setting the people hear the message of Fatima repeated: prayer, works of penance, and recourse to the Immaculate Heart of Mary.

Holy Mass is offered frequently every day. Thousands receive Holy Communion. Confessions are heard continuously, and people pray the Rosary. In 1982, when he visited the Shrine at Fatima, John Paul II said:

"The Church has always taught . . . that God's revelation was brought to completion in Jesus Christ . . . and that no new public revelation is to be expected before the glorious manifestation of Our Lord. The Church has accepted the message of Fatima, above all because that message contains a truth and a call . . . of the Gospel itself."

Special devotions are held at the Basilica.

Through Mary to Jesus

The apparitions at Fatima remind us that although Mary is Queen of Heaven, she is deeply concerned with her children on earth. Her mission is to lead us to her Son. When we honor her, we show our love for Jesus Who made her so beautiful and holy.

We should answer our Lady's requests at Fatima by showing great love for her Son especially in the Eucharist. Also we should consecrate ourselves to her Immaculate Heart, and pray the Rosary.

By doing what Mary, our Heavenly Mother, asks, we can be sure of drawing close to Jesus and attaining eternal life.

MAGNIFICENT EDITIONS THAT BELONG IN EVERY CATHOLIC HOME

FIRST MASS BOOK—Ideal Children's Mass Book with all the official Mass prayers. Colored illustrations of the Mass and the Life of Christ. Confession and Communion Prayers. **Ask for No. 808**

PICTURE BOOK OF SAINTS—By Rev. L. Lovasik, S.V.D. Illustrated Lives of the Saints in full color for Young and Old. It clearly depicts the lives of over 100 popular Saints in word and picture. **Ask for No. 235**

MY FIRST PRAYERBOOK—By Rev. Lawrence G. Lovasik, S.V.D. Beautiful new prayerbook that provides prayers for the main occasions in a child's life. Features simple language, easy-to-read type, and full-color illustrations. **Ask for No. 205**

THE MASS FOR CHILDREN—By Rev. Jude Winkler, OFM Conv. New beautifully illustrated Mass Book that explains the Mass to children and contains the Mass responses they should know. It is sure to help children know and love the Mass. **Ask for No. 215**

LIVES OF THE SAINTS—New Revised Edition. Short life of a Saint and prayer for every day of the year. Over 50 illustrations. Ideal for daily meditation and private study. **Ask for No. 870**

CATHOLIC PICTURE BIBLE—By Rev. L. Lovasik, S.V.D. Thrilling, inspiring and educational for all ages. Over 110 Bible stories retold in simple words, and illustrated in full color. **Ask for No. 435**

St. Joseph FIRST CHILDREN'S BIBLE—By Father Lovasik, S.V.D. Over 50 of the best-loved stories of the Bible retold for children. Each story is written in clear and simple language and illustrated by an attractive and superbly inspiring illustration. A perfect book for introducing very young children to the Bible. **Ask for No. 135**

The STORY OF JESUS—By Father Lovasik, S.V.D. A large-format book with magnificent full colored pictures for young readers to enjoy and learn about the life of Jesus. Each story is told in simple and direct words. **Ask for No. 535**

WHEREVER CATHOLIC BOOKS ARE SOLD